W9-AZU-622

TUBA CITY AGENCY
BUREAU OF INDIAN AFFAIRS

DE SOTO

Finder of the Mississippi

Lee

Bro Dert

1973

3274

DE SOTO
FINDER OF THE MISSISSIPPI

By RONALD SYME

Illustrated by WILLIAM STOBBS

WILLIAM MORROW AND COMPANY
New York   1957

© 1957 by William Morrow and Company, Inc. All Rights Reserved.

Published simultaneously in the Dominion of Canada by George J. McLeod
Limited, Toronto. Printed in the United States of America.

Library of Congress Catalog Card Number: 57-5061

10   11   12   13   14   15   75   74   73   72   71

The lonely road wound southward across the mountains of central Spain. From an open window, high in the strong stone walls of his father's house, young Hernando de Soto could see along the dusty track for several miles.

When he was ten years old, in the year 1510, few travelers ever used that highway. Hernando used to spend much of his time watching the green countryside, dotted with grazing sheep, and the shadows passing swiftly across the ripening fields of golden wheat.

Two or three years later, Hernando noticed that more people were beginning to pass daily along the road. Instead of some wealthy landowner on a richly saddled horse, or a laborer on his way to the fields, there now came parties of horsemen, and groups of sturdy young countrymen on foot. They were all going toward the south. Hernando wondered if they would travel far enough to reach the green vineyards in the province of Andalusia, and the famous seaport town of Cadiz. It was three hundred miles to Cadiz, which was much farther than he had ever been, but Hernando knew that Christopher Columbus had sailed from that harbor on his later voyages to the New World. Why, he wondered, were so many strangers going in the direction of Cadiz and the sea?

"They are eager to reach the New World," his father told him. "The story has spread throughout Spain that in the great countries Columbus discovered there is gold in plenty; aye, and unlimited rich land for everyone, too."

Hernando thought for a little while. He was a slender, rather silent boy who liked listening better than talking. "You do not believe the stories about gold, sire?" he asked.

"The news may be true," said his father, frowning slightly. "But the departure of all these people can bring only misfortune to Spain. Already a shortage of labor is coming to our countryside. Look at those fields of unreaped wheat. Walk along yonder valley and you will see how the stone-walled irrigation ditches are falling into ruin. Now that our Spanish workers are leaving for the New World, there will soon be few farms left in Castile, and ruin will come to Spain."

Hernando remembered what his father had said. From now on it grieved him to see that the crowds of men passing along the road toward Cadiz never grew less. By the time Hernando had become a tall young man of twenty-one, ruin was coming to the countryside. When the wind blew strongly, clouds of dust arose from hillsides where sheep had once grazed. Now the travelers moving southward during the spring and summer months grew in numbers with every year that passed; for nothing but hardship was approaching as the wealth of the countryside decreased. And the estate belonging to Hernando's own family was nearing its end.

"From what we have heard, there is both wealth and poverty in the New World," he said to his father. "But only poverty awaits us here. Give me leave, sire, to make for Cadiz and the lands that Columbus discovered."

"I will not stop you," replied his father, "for

you speak the truth. Go now, if you wish; it is better not to waste the years."

In the year 1523, Hernando de Soto rode off along the road where so many others had passed already. With sword and armor and a few gold pieces, he was going to seek his fortune somewhere in the New World.

Like most vessels reaching the Caribbean Sea from Spain, the ship which bore Hernando made for the island of Hispaniola. This was where newcomers got their first glimpse of the growing Spanish empire in America. The sight was disappointing for them. During the thirty years the Spaniards had been in Hispaniola, they had destroyed the beauty of the island. Most of the glorious forests had been chopped down to build houses and bridges. Hillsides were covered with crumbling holes and ugly trenches where men had dug vainly to find gold.

The few Carib natives still alive were thin, ragged, and wretched. The Spaniards treated them with cruelty and scorn. The town of San Domingo was a sprawling, dirty, and sun-baked slum, where ragged men gambled for pennies and cursed the day they had come to the New World.

13

Hernando was a shrewd young man. After one glance at Hispaniola he knew that only starvation awaited him there. Without grumbling over his disappointment, he boarded another ship and sailed across the Caribbean Sea to the mainland. With other men he tramped many miles to the Pacific Ocean and the newly founded city of Panama.

The population of Panama were excited over some recent news. A black-bearded adventurer named Francisco Pizarro was talking about making a voyage southward into unknown seas to search for a mysterious land of gold. He had found two ships. Now he needed sailors and fighting men to go with him. They were much harder to find, for Pizarro promised no rewards. If he discovered gold, then his companions would share it with him. If they were all killed by Indians, it would be no worse than enduring poverty and starvation in overcrowded Panama.

Francisco Pizarro and his bold company of penniless men sailed in 1524. On board one of the leaky
and worm-eaten little ships went tall, wiry, silent
Hernando de Soto.

A thousand miles south of Panama, Pizarro
found the great Inca kingdom of Peru. After storms
and starvation, he and his two hundred followers
had come to the land of gold. They fought for
nearly ten years as they advanced slowly into the

16

great and beautiful country. As fast as they defeated one Inca army, another faced them.

Gradually the senior officers of the Spanish army began to hear the name of Hernando de Soto. It was Hernando who always seemed to be in command of the Spanish scouts advancing in front of the main army. And finally, it was Hernando who led an advance party into the treasure-filled city of Cuzco, which lay high in the inland mountains.

17

TUBA CITY AGENCY
BUREAU OF INDIAN AFFAIRS

When the whole kingdom of Peru crashed at last in ruins, Pizarro showed his gratitude. There was gold in plenty for every man in his army, but some of the finest jewelry went to Hernando de Soto. He returned to Spain as a lean, sun-darkened veteran of thirty-six. Men said he was a daring and fearless soldier. Now there were menservants riding behind him along the road to Castile. Hernando reached home with memories of one of the greatest adventures in the history of the world, and a fortune valued at a million dollars.

Life seemed dull in the quiet old house beside the mountain road. Within a few months of his return Hernando became restless. Fresh dreams were stirring in his mind. He had no wish to return to Peru, where the Spanish *conquistadores*, or men of the victorious army, were fighting among themselves over the division of land and gold. Hernan-

18

do's thoughts were turning northward to an almost unknown country, recently named *La Florida*, because it had been discovered on Easter Day (*Pasqua Florida*). A toothless and half-crazy Spanish officer, Juan Ponce de Leon, had chanced to find the coast about the year 1513. He returned eight years later and died of an arrow wound he received on the beach.

A year later the ship of a Spanish sea captain named Miruelo was blown onto the coast of Florida. The Indians treated him kindly and he returned to Hispaniola without having lost any men. On hearing what Miruelo had to say, a gang of Spanish slave hunters sailed for Florida. They kidnaped a hundred and thirty Indians, all of whom died, and they themselves were nearly drowned during the voyage back to Hispaniola.

The Indian tribes grimly swore revenge for the treacherous kidnaping of their fellow tribesmen.

The last Spaniard to land in Florida was De Narváez, who went there in 1528. His little army managed to get a long way into Florida before hunger, tomahawks, and swamp fever destroyed them. Only four men returned alive to Hispaniola, and De Narváez was not among them. One of the four survivors said that the interior of Florida was covered with fine groves of timber and had vast meadows of rich soil. But what he said about the Indians scared off all the other Spaniards who were looking for fresh territory to seize.

In Peru we made the mistake of treating the Indians cruelly, thought Hernando. Even where there was no need, we greatly hurt or killed them. That was why they turned and fought against us with such fury. Spaniards have made the same mistake in Florida. If I went there I would try to show the Indians that I wished to be friends with them. Afterward they might let us explore the country in peace.

The occupation and settlement of Florida became a great dream in Hernando's mind. He longed to march again across a strange and unexplored country. In Florida there would be adventure, and fertile soil for Spanish farms. Perhaps there would be gold and silver with which to pay for the building of new towns and harbors, as Pizarro had done in Peru.

King Charles V of Spain knew a lot about valiant young Hernando de Soto. He had read the accounts of the conquest of Peru which Pizarro had written. But he was also inclined to be miserly, except in raising money to fight the neighboring countries of Europe.

"You have my leave to occupy Florida," he said. "You shall be governor of whatever part of the

country you choose. You must pay all the costs of your expedition, so it is only right that you should be given fresh titles and rewards."

By the spring of 1537 Hernando had seven large ships and three small ones lying beside stone quays in the Spanish port of San Lucar. Into their massive holds went coils of rope, barrels of salted meat, baskets of preserved oranges, dates, and figs, kegs of nails, ingots of iron, and sawn timber for building purposes. Hernando was a quick but careful planner. He overlooked nothing he might need for an army or a colony somewhere in Florida.

News of his expedition spread quickly throughout Spain.

Here, thought the people, is another great opportunity to find new lands and wealth for ourselves. Hernando de Soto is one of the youngest and bravest captains of Spain. Surely he will conquer Florida, as Cortes conquered Mexico and Pizarro conquered Peru.

Younger sons of noble families hurried to San Lucar. So did sixty of the hard-faced *conquistadores* who had returned from Peru. Wealthy men, rich in armor and with servants of their own, also came, as well as sturdy, simple-minded peasants who owned nothing but the earth-stained clothes they wore.

Hernando knew there would be hard times in Florida. He chose only the younger volunteers. Of all his nine hundred and fifty men, only one–a battled-scarred old soldier named Juan Mateos–had gray hair.

The proud and glittering expedition to Florida sailed from San Lucar in April, 1538. The Spaniards were valiant soldiers, but they had little skill as sailors. Two of their ships collided on the first night out. Hernando, in a cold and deadly rage, almost hanged the offending captain. Later in the voyage two soldiers started fighting over an argument in a card game. They fell overboard and were drowned. A greyhound which tumbled overside was luckier. After swimming for five hours, it was picked up by a ship that happened to be passing. Next morning the owner of the dog fell into the sea and was lost. Finally, on entering the harbor of Santiago in Cuba, Hernando's own vessel, the *San*

Christòbal, hit an underwater reef and nearly smashed her hull. When all the ships were riding safely at anchor, soldiers and sailors hurried ashore to kneel down and pray with gratitude because the voyage was ended.

Hernando stayed almost a year in Cuba. He sent one of his best navigators to explore the coast of Florida and find a good harbor, where his fleet could shelter while unloading men and supplies. Meanwhile, he started buying four hundred good horses, of which there were plenty in Cuba.

"If the Indians in Florida are like the Incas in Peru," he said, "they will not worry about our foot soldiers. They will fear only our armored cavalry."

The captain who had gone to explore the coast of Florida returned to Santiago. "We have found a good harbor on the west coast," he said. "All our ships can anchor safely in it, and there is a good beach for landing troops and cargo."

The horses were loaded into the vessels. So were three hundred pigs, which Hernando decided would be useful in the new country. A few extra volunteers also marched aboard, increasing the number of soldiers to a thousand.

Hernando's fleet sailed for Florida at the end of May, 1539. Nineteen days later, after a cold and rough voyage, the ships dropped anchor in the harbor, which they christened the Bay of the Holy Spirit (Tampa Bay). As the boats began to ferry men and horses, pigs and cargo ashore, Hernando leaned over the side and gazed at the dark green coast line. Forests reached almost to the water's edge. There seemed to be low and marshy country farther inland. There was no sign of Indians or any other living creature.

The soldiers were all ashore, and most of the cargo had been landed, when the Indian warriors attacked through the gray mist of early dawn. They

came leaping and running, wild and muscular fig-
ures covered with war paint, before the startled
Spaniards were clear of the blankets in which they
had slept. Armed with tomahawks, arrows, and
scalping knives, the warriors burst into the camp.
Shouting with alarm, the Spaniards grabbed swords
and lances to fight for their scalps. They were
forced back by the horde of slashing and stabbing
warriors until they were standing in the shallow
water of the beach. Reinforcements started piling
ashore from the ships, and cavaliers swung themselves onto hastily saddled horses. Quickly the Indians turned and ran for the forest. They left
behind them wounded and frightened soldiers, and
a horse dead from an arrow driven with such terrible force that the shaft had gone through its heart.

"These are wilder and more terrible fighters than
the men of Peru," Hernando said thoughtfully.
"It will be hard to find friends among them."

He found help in an unexpected way. Out from the woods came a brown-skinned man wearing an Indian waistcloth and carrying a finely polished longbow and a quiver of flint-tipped arrows. All one side of the stranger's body was terribly scarred by ancient wounds, which the Spaniards shuddered to see.

"My name is Juan Ortiz, sire," declared the man. He spoke in slow and awkward Spanish. "I was a soldier with the explorer, De Narváez, when he came to this country ten years ago. Some Indians captured me. Their chief, a wretch named Hirri-higua, tortured me for a year and a half. He wished to kill me, but his wife and three young daughters pleaded for my life. These scars on my body were caused when I was half-roasted over red-hot stones. When I recovered from my burns, one of the young girls helped me to escape to the province of a young and kind chieftain named Mucozo. He has pro-

tected me from Hirrihigua for eight years. Now he has sent me to say that he wishes to be friends with you. There are friendly Indians nearby who will carry back any message you wish to send to Mucozo."

"I send him my greetings," Hernando replied. "Tell him we are eager to be his friends. He has nothing to fear from us. We will not harm his people, nor steal any of the food they may have planted for their own use."

Juan Ortiz remained with the Spaniards. Hernando treated him generously, supplying him with clothes, money, and bedding. From then on, poor Juan Ortiz became Hernando's most valuable interpreter.

A few days later, young Mucozo himself came to see Hernando. "Do not try to reach the heart of this country," he advised. "There are great swamps on the way, where the Indians will certainly ambush you. Settle in this district, which belongs to me. There is room enough for all of you. I will give you acres of land."

Hernando shook his head. "No," he said. "I am grateful to you, Mucozo, but I wish to see all this country of Florida. One day, perhaps, we shall return to live in friendship with you."

One hundred and twenty Spaniards were left to guard the supplies on the beach at Tampa Bay. The four larger ships began refilling their water casks for the voyage back to Cuba. Hernando decided to keep only the three smaller vessels in Tampa Bay. With nearly nine hundred men, he began marching away from the coast.

The wondering Spaniards passed through flourishing groves of walnut and mulberry, cherry trees, pines, and live oaks. Sometimes the path wound across sunny meadows where the grass was tall and sweet, and unknown birds sang in green thickets. But always on their flanks, the Indians crept and watched and waited.

Hernando came to the first swamp. His men saw stagnant pools of water, evil with the smell of rotting wood, and treacherous surfaces of black earth, covered with a slimy green moss. Tangled groves of live-oak trees made perfect hiding places for an

enemy. Through the center of the swamp, which was three miles wide, flowed a stream too deep to wade. It measured about ninety feet across. Indians had felled two trees so that their trunks lay side by side. Across them they had lashed pieces of wood to form a bridge.

Hernando led the way into the bubbling mud. Horses and soldiers struggled through chest-high

slime. They were almost at the deepest part when the air was filled with a deadly whistling sound. From among the trees hundreds of arrows fell on the struggling Spaniards.

The way to the bridge was choked with heavy branches and masses of driftwood. Hernando ordered two soldiers to clear a path for the horses with their axes. The army stood and waited in the falling shower of arrows while the two men went forward. They cleared away the litter, but were hit and wounded by arrows while they worked. The army crossed the stream into shallower water.

The Spaniards could not attack the almost invisible Indians. Horses were useless in the mud and water; crossbows could not be reloaded except on dry ground. A couple of hundred soldiers carried primitive muskets. These clumsy weapons weighed eighteen pounds, could fire at the rate of only one shot a minute, and had a range of not more than fifty yards. Like the crossbows, they could not be used now.

The army reached dry ground beyond the swamp. Hernando gazed at his mud-stained, wet, and exhausted men. One soldier had an arrow through his neck; others were wounded about the face. The water had protected the bodies of the men from flying arrows, but several of the horses

had been deeply pierced by the bone-tipped shafts.

"These arrows are fiercer than those of Peru,"
Hernando said. "The Inca troops did not have the
strength to draw longbows so powerful. Some of
these shafts will penetrate even our good steel
armor."

In the baggage which the army had left on the
coast there were heavy jackets of pleated cotton,
about three inches thick. Hernando saw that his

men must wear this protective clothing. The cavalry could cover the bodies of their horses with layers of blankets stitched together. It would be foolish to go any farther without protecting both men and horses. So he sent a strong party of cavalry back through the swamp to fetch the heavy coats.

Miles beyond the great swamp, the Spaniards reached territory belonging to a chieftain named Acuera. Hernando sent a message of greeting to him. "We have not come to harm your people or damage your villages," he said. "I ask only permission to go with my men through your country."

A friendly Indian, whom Juan Ortiz had taught to speak Spanish, brought back Acuera's reply.

"I have heard of you Spaniards, who earn a living by robbing, destroying, and murdering people. I want no friendship with men such as you. I have ordered my warriors to bring me two Spanish scalps every week. If you have any sense, you will go away quickly before you die beneath our toma-hawks."

The Spaniards remained twenty days in Acuera's territory. The warriors of the forest were near them all the time. Any man who wandered even a hundred yards from the camp was killed and scalped before other soldiers could come to his aid.

Beyond Acuera's province the forests grew lighter and the ground rolled upward from the swamps. Hernando gazed at radiant stretches of countryside, where the horses cropped unending grass and found shade in pleasant groves of pine and walnut. The Indians were less warlike in this region. They fled from their villages when they learned that the Spaniards were coming. Soldiers entered their houses, some of them made of bark from trees, some of cleverly braided reeds encased in mud. They seized corn and vegetables, prunes, raisins, and acorns wherever they found them.

41

Hernando could not stop their looting. The men
were hungry, and the army's food supplies were
running short. Yet with cold discipline he still ordered them to treat all prisoners kindly. "We did
not come to this country to make enemies," he said.
"Perhaps in time the Indians will believe our word
when we tell them we want nothing but their
friendship."

Hernando would have chosen wisely if he had decided to stay in this fertile district. But he was a natural explorer, always eager to see what lay beyond the next river, or on the other side of a hill. There was something almost magical about the great forests and the bright grasslands of Florida. He knew his army must go onward with him until he had seen much more of this vast country.

At last they came to the Ocala River, and crossed it. Now they were in territory far beyond that which any other European had seen. Every now and then they met some friendly tribe, but much more often they were attacked by enemies.

In Vitachuco, a district north of the Ocala River, ten thousand warriors in war paint and magnificent feather headdresses waited to destroy the Spaniards. This time the Indians left their forests and attacked across the open prairie. It was a bad mistake, for they had no steel spears with which to face the

cavalry. Three hundred and fifty Spanish horsemen charged the Indian ranks. Arrows could not
pierce their heavy jerkins and armor. Their lances
and swords were more deadly than tomahawks or
wooden spears.

The Indians broke and ran. Several thousand of
them reached safety in the forest. Nearly a thousand others fled into a small lake. Being out of their
depth, they had to start swimming, while Spanish
troops surrounded the banks. Even now, however,
the warriors would not surrender. While two or
three of them swam side by side, another would
climb onto their backs and fire an arrow at the
Spaniards. They kept it up all night. By dawn next
morning, only fifty of them had surrendered. The
others were still swimming, after sixteen hours in
the water.

Hernando grew sorry for them. He could not
bear the thought of leaving such gallant men to

drown. "Bring our prisoners to the water's edge," he said. "Tell them to call to their friends in the water and say that we have treated them well."

Hernando's plan was successful. By afternoon nine hundred Indians had come ashore, after swimming for twenty-four hours. Only seven warriors remained in the lake. They were growing weak and could only just keep themselves afloat. Hernando's heart was bursting with pity. "Get our best swimmers to go in and drag them out," he said. "I will not stand here and see brave lives wasted in this manner."

The Indians were hauled out of the water, where they had spent so many hours. Four of them were about thirty-five years old, the other three not more than eighteen. After they had rested and eaten, Hernando went to see them. He asked why they preferred death to surrender.

"We promised our chieftain we would defeat

your army or die," one of the warriors said. "We lost the battle, so now we seek only death. If you wish to do us a kindness, order your men to kill us with their swords."

Hernando refused. He saw that all seven men were given as much food as they could eat.

"And after seven days," said one of the Spaniards in the army, "Captain De Soto gave these warriors presents of cloth, and mirrors, and other things from Spain. He sent them to their homes, together with a few other Indians of the tribe who had been taken prisoner in the fighting."

The Spaniards kept about nine hundred Indians captive. Hernando thought they seemed grateful that their lives had been spared. He planned to use them as porters and servants for his army. The Spaniards had done this successfully in Peru, but Hernando still did not realize just how different these Indians were from the milder Incas.

Vitachuco, the chieftain, was among the prisoners. He was a tall and powerful man. Although unarmed, he was still determined to destroy the Spaniards. Secretly he ordered each of his warriors to kill one Spaniard when the signal was given.

Hernando invited Vitachuco to sit beside him at meals. One morning the chief stretched out his arms and shook them with tremendous force. The Indians of Florida often did this before attempting some great act of strength. Then, standing up, Vitachuco caught Hernando by the collar with his left hand and hit him a frightful blow with his right fist. Taken by complete surprise Hernando fell backward, unconscious. Screaming a war cry that was heard all over the camp, Vitachuco leapt at Hernando to kill him outright. The other Spaniards grabbed their swords. They killed the chief before he reached their captain, and he died, still yelling his signal to the warriors.

All nine hundred Indians heard it. They had no weapons of their own; but they seized blazing logs, stones, sticks, heavy jugs, and pans of boiling water. They attacked the Spaniards with these things. Noise and fighting broke out all over the camp. A number of men were killed. Others were badly hurt by the queer weapons. The soldiers grabbed their swords and killed every single warrior of Vitachuco's tribe.

This wild and treacherous revolt made Hernando's men hate and fear the Indians more than ever. They never trusted any Indian warriors again. Only Hernando's order prevented them from treating prisoners much more cruelly in future, and they began to disobey him now whenever they got a chance.

The army marched northward for another sixty miles and came to a place named Apalachee. Here they found wide meadows, planted with corn and beans. This open country was fairly safe, but the nearby forests were full of enemies.

Hernando hesitated for a little while. Shall I go on? he wondered. Or shall I remain here? Sixty men have died already, and we have lost some horses. The Indians are learning how to attack us. They aim their arrows at our legs, which are unprotected by armor, and they are determined to kill all our horses. When we have no cavalry left, they will swamp us by their numbers. Even now they are starting to take cover under low-branched trees where our horsemen cannot reach them. In Peru, the Incas were willing to surrender when they saw that a battle was lost. These Indians are ready to die if they can first kill one of us or slay a horse. Surrender means only one thing to them. They consider it a disgrace.

Hernando gradually made up his mind. He would go on still farther, hoping to find some other fertile district, where the Indians were peaceful. But now October had arrived and the nights were growing cold. He decided to spend the winter in this corner of Florida. He sent for one of his bravest officers, Juan de Anasco, and told him to lead a small party of cavalry back to Tampa. He was to order the ships to sail northward to the coast of Apalachee Bay. This would bring them within a few miles of Hernando's winter camp. The one hundred and twenty men who were left to guard the stores would march overland through Florida until they came to Apalachee. The three little ships were not big enough to take men and stores as well. Hernando knew that with a stronger army he could go on marching through the country when the spring of 1540 came.

Juan de Anasco made the long journey back to Tampa. He knew that the only chance of safety for his party was to travel faster than the news of their

coming could reach the tribes on the way. They rode from daybreak to dark. They kept away from villages, swam rivers on horseback, and nearly froze to death while wading through swamps. One of them, twenty-year-old Juan Cacho, was so numbed by cold for several days that he had to be tied to his horse like a wooden statue. Juan de Anasco and his companions finished the journey in eleven days, one of which was spent in crossing the worst swamp they had yet encountered.

The good chieftain, Mucozo, and his whole tribe helped the Spaniards to load the ships. The vessels sailed for Apalachee Bay, and the rest of the men started their journey through the swamps and forests to join Hernando at the northern end of Florida. They arrived in December, a hungry, exhausted, unshaven band of men in rusty armor, who had fought the Indians almost every step of the way.

"Sail westward along this coast," Hernando had said to the captains of the ships. "Try to find a good harbor where we can spend next winter."

The captains sailed back with good news. Two hundred miles farther on, they had found a sheltered and pleasant harbor which the Indians called Achusi (Pensacola).

"Now go back to Cuba," said Hernando. "In

October of this year of 1540, we will meet you
again in Achusi. Bring crossbows, muskets, and
padded cotton jerkins; also shoes and clothing for
my men. After another year in Florida, we shall
badly need such things."

The ships sailed away, and some of Hernando's
men looked enviously after them. They were dis-
appointed with Florida. They had found no gold or

silver—only hunger and hardship and dangerous enemies. Now they were alone in Florida, and cut off from the outside world. They would have to spend the winter in a dreary fort made of timber and earth. Their only cheerful thought was that within its walls they would be safe from the arrows and scalping knives.

A cold, wet spring came to Florida. Hernando marched out of the camp and began leading his men in a westerly direction. They traveled quickly, pausing only to fight when necessary. During the winter they had heard that in a nearby province named Cofachiqui there was plenty of gold and silver. The news caused their spirits to rise.

Perhaps, they thought, we are like the army Pizarro led. They, too, found much hardship and suffering before they came to the region of gold in Peru.

The countryside was bare of food, the rivers were in flood, and Indian storehouses were empty of grain. The Spaniards lived on the tendrils of young vines, roots, and small birds and animals which their Indian companions managed to trap or kill. Hunger forced them to eat many of the pigs Hernando had brought from Cuba. These animals were thriving in Florida and increasing in numbers.

Finally the Spaniards reached Cofachiqui, which they described as "a pretty country, sheltered from the sun by vast forests of mulberry trees and other trees heavy with fruit." It lay in the modern state of Georgia.

The ruler of Cofachiqui was a young and pretty Indian girl. She fearlessly came to see Hernando, and greeted him as a friend.

"I will order houses in the village to be prepared for you and your officers," she said. "My people will build huts with branches and grass, where your men will be sheltered from both the sun and the rain."

The Spaniards marveled at the beauty and graceful manner of this young girl. They christened her the Lady of Cofachiqui, and treated her with great politeness. Here at last, they said, was someone they could trust. Eagerly they showed her gold and silver rings.

Were there any metals like these in her country, they asked.

"If this is all you came here for," the girl replied, "I will get some of my people to bring you great baskets full of it."

The Indians returned, bringing heavy loads on their backs. The greediest of the Spaniards raced to meet them. They emptied the contents of the baskets onto the ground and grabbed handfuls for themselves. They found they were looking at copper ore and a worthless, silvery material called iron pyrites. There was not a trace of gold in any of the baskets.

Yet, in Cofachiqui, Hernando's men found wealth of another kind. The princess told them to enter a great burial temple of her people, which stood on a hillside. There they found woven baskets piled high with splendid pearls. They reckoned there were several tons of this treasure.

"Leave the pearls where they are," said Hernando. "We have a long way yet to go, and there is no sense in burdening ourselves with useless loads. Every man may take two handfuls and no more than that."

Hernando saw something else in the temple which would be of more use to his army. There were bales of beautifully cured deerskins. "I would ask you to give us some of these," he said to the Lady of Cofachiqui. "The brambles in the thickets and the rivers we must wade are ruining what clothes we have."

The young princess agreed. When the army marched out of her village, some of the men were dressed in buckskin shirts and trousers.

Out of Georgia and into South Carolina went Hernando and his men. The Spaniards described it as a "level and pleasant country with little rivers flowing ten or twelve miles apart. We saw few

mountains, but good grass on which cattle would fatten."

Since leaving Tampa Bay, the army had covered about a thousand miles on foot, but still Hernando was not satisfied. He longed to find the perfect locality in which to build his settlement. He believed that somewhere ahead must lie a region better than anything he had already seen. By July, he was exploring in North Carolina.

The summer came to an end. The vessels would be arriving soon in Pensacola Bay. Hernando turned southwestward in order to reach the coast. Behind him went seven hundred Spaniards—lean, bearded, sun-darkened men in battered armor and tattered clothing. Three hundred had died since leaving Tampa Bay; a couple of others had deserted. The horses now numbered less than three hundred.

After passing through Tennessee, the Spanish

army entered Alabama on their way to the coast.
The tribes in its northern half were men of great
height and strength, but not of a warlike nature.
The weary Spaniards were given friendly greetings
in the villages and supplied with fruit and corn. As
they ate and slept in peace, they remembered
thankfully that they had done little fighting all that
summer. Their captain's good treatment of the In-

dians seemed at last to be earning a just reward.

They came to Mauvila, a village on the banks of a wide river. Less than a hundred wooden houses stood inside a surrounding wall, which was eighteen feet high and made of tree trunks plastered with mud. Each of these houses was a couple of hundred feet in length. Inside them waited twelve thousand warriors. Tascaluza, the giant chieftain of the tribe, had been boasting that he would destroy the Spanish army. Now he was ready to do it. His warriors all knew they must remain hidden until Tascaluza gave the signal.

Half of the Spanish army made their camp outside the towering wall of the village. Hernando and his officers were invited to occupy a few small huts inside Mauvila.

Tascaluza waited until the Spaniards had laid aside their armor and weapons to eat the succotash and fruit placed before them.

Then, secretly, he made a sign.

Out from the barnlike houses burst naked Indians in full war paint. Several thousand of them raced through the entrance gates to attack the soldiers encamped on the meadows. The rest headed for the cottages where Hernando and his companions were seated.

Many of the cavalrymen had no time to mount their horses. They fought on foot, with ax and sword and dagger. When the Indians saw that most of their fiercest arrows failed to pierce the quilted jackets worn by the soldiers, they used their heavy war bows as clubs. They struck with such tremendous force that some of the Spaniards were killed by the blows and others had their steel helmets cracked open.

Hernando managed to reach his horse and climb into the saddle. An arrow struck him in the upper leg and its point reached the bone. He broke off the

shaft, told none of his friends he was wounded, and rode into the center of the village. There he tried to rally the scared and retreating soldiers. He set them an example by galloping his horse at the hordes of warriors and clearing a path through them with his sword.

During the fight the entire village caught fire. Spaniards and Indians rolled in waves through smoke and flames and dust, stabbing, thrusting, and slashing as they went. Wounded men were burned to death or trampled by the horses. Dying Indians grabbed the legs of Spanish soldiers and brought them to the ground, where they were clubbed or stabbed before they could regain their feet.

Hernando, his lean face blackened by smoke, his hair and beard scorched by flames, steadied the army. Slowly the Spaniards began to drive back the Indian masses. The warriors called on their women to assist them. Out of the blazing houses and down the streets came hundreds of fierce-faced women, swinging tomahawks as valiantly as the men. The battle went on all day, from nine in the morning until sunset. By that time the village was in utter ruins. Several thousand warriors lay dead in the streets and among them lay sixty-nine Spaniards. Forty-five of the precious horses were killed, and many others wounded. The flames destroyed most

71

of the army's medical supplies, reserves of food, stores of weapons, kegs of nails, clothing, and saddlery. Half-dead with exhaustion and bleeding from wounds, the Spaniards made a rough camp for the night outside the lifeless village. Only a few of the warriors escaped into the forest, and they took with them the women. Among these fugitives was the chieftain Tascaluza, who had planned the destruction.

Perhaps when Hernando inspected his broken, bleeding and discouraged army, he knew that his attempt to win Florida had failed. Even his officers were overcome with horror by the battle. They began to mutter that they must escape quickly from this treacherous country. Only death would come to them if they stayed in America.

An Indian messenger brought news to Juan Ortiz that the three ships had returned to Pensacola and were awaiting Hernando. Now the whole army thought only of reaching the harbor. The vessels could carry all of them back to Cuba in a couple of voyages.

Hernando heard what his officers and men were saying. He knew they were right, but his proud spirit would not allow him to return to Cuba in defeat. Somehow, he might yet find a way to better fortune.

Three weeks after the battle of Mauvila, he gave the order to march.

"We will not go toward the coast," he told his dismayed followers, "for it would be the action of a coward to leave this country now. We will march *away* from the sea and onward to the west."

Through Alabama and into Mississippi went six hundred Spaniards. It was now the winter of 1540. Snow was drifting across the prairie when they reached the abandoned Indian town of Chicasaw.

In the nearby forests of walnut and oak, warriors awaited an opportunity to attack.

In January a high wind at midnight gave the Indians their chance. They rushed the town, using torches and flaming arrows to set the thatched huts alight. The Spaniards fought for two hours before the tribe was satisfied with the death and destruction they had brought to Hernando and his men. They slipped back into the forest, leaving forty Spaniards and fifty horses dead on the frozen ground. One arrow, driven with terrible force, had gone right through a horse's shoulder and come halfway out on the other side.

Warmer weather came in April, 1541. Hernando left the ruined village behind. In May he reached the banks of the largest river his army had seen in America. The Indian name for it was Chucagua, but the Spaniards called it the Rio Grande, or Great River, and gazed in amazement at its mile-

wide stream. (Its name today is the Mississippi River.)

Heavy forests grew on both banks and the water flowed between steep and towering cliffs. The Spaniards halted for three weeks and made wooden barges in which to ferry themselves across the Great River.

The army marched onward through Arkansas during the rest of the long, hot summer. They fought as they went, ate corn whenever they came to a friendly village, and lived for the rest of the time on deer and other game they killed. For a while they ran short of salt, and this brought a new sickness, and even death, to them. Friendly Indians led the way to natural salt deposits in the hills. So great was the Spaniards' hunger for salt that they actually ate handfuls of it.

In eastern Arkansas they found bison meat in Indian villages. They never saw the herds, and wondered greatly where such excellent meat came from. They also marveled at the size and warmth of the buffalo robes they saw in the deserted houses of the people.

Hernando knew it would be wiser to turn back toward the Mississippi. He was worried about the three ships which had come to Pensacola to meet him, for he knew that by this time their captains would be searching for him along the coast. And yet, whenever daylight came, he said to himself, Today we will march a little farther in search of fresh wonders.

The fall came, and then winter drew near. Now it was too late to begin the homeward march. Hernando chose the Indian town of Utiangue in southeast Arkansas in which to await the spring of 1542. The surrounding countryside contained several creeks. There was corn in the storehouses, and the neighboring forests held plenty of rabbits and deer.

The Spaniards rejoiced at the thought of spending a warm, comfortable, and well-fed winter.

But when some of the officers looked at Hernando, they grew worried. "His face is growing thin," they said. "He does not laugh and joke with us as much as he used to. Pray heaven nothing happens to our captain; for if it does, we are lost."

Hernando had plenty to think about, and his thoughts were not cheerful. Only five hundred men were left of the thousand who had landed at Tampa Bay two and a half years ago. One hundred and fifty horses remained of the three hundred and fifty he had brought from Cuba. One more battle like Mauvila might destroy his weakened army.

I have found no gold, he thought, as he sat gazing into the log fire on winter evenings. Nor have I obtained any other treasure to replace the fortune I spent on fitting out this expedition. Five hundred good Spaniards have died for nothing. Yet perhaps

there is enough time left to found a settlement in this great and fruitful country. If I can only return to the plain near Achusi, we can build a little colony. Help will come to us from Cuba and Hispaniola, where men are hungry for land as good as this. Yes, when spring comes we will go back to the Great River and return by sea to Achusi.

To make sure that no more promising country

lay ahead, Hernando again marched a short distance westward in the spring of 1542. His soldiers trod the soil of the future state of Louisiana. Juan Ortiz, the interpreter, died, and Hernando was saddened by the loss of this valuable man. He gave the order to begin the homeward journey.

"We will build ships and sail down the Great River to the sea," he told his men. "When we reach the ocean, we will turn eastward and go to Achusi. Instead of gold, we will reward ourselves with rich fields and farms. The people of Hispaniola and Cuba will be glad to buy all the food we can grow."

Back across Louisiana went the ragged, hungry, and sun-browned men. Some limped as they walked, for the clumsy sandals they wore were of little use to their feet on stony ground. Their armor was tarnished and rusty, and they had scant protection from rain or burning sunshine.

Because of their haste to reach the Mississippi, the

Spaniards traveled fast. When the Indian tribes left them alone, they sometimes covered thirty miles between dawn and sunset. On and on they went, during the late spring and early summer. At the beginning of June they saw the high banks of the Mississippi ahead of them. Thankfully they camped beside the river and prepared to build their ships. The local tribe was friendly and treated them in a kindly manner.

"Give them presents," said Hernando. "Tell them to bring resin from the pine trees in the forest, and such cordage as they make from the skins of animals. We shall need many things to build our ships, and we must all share in the work."

Hernando never finished this last great task. He had fought too long and tired himself too much. In every battle he had led his men against the enemy. He had spent whole nights visiting sentries and watching over the wounded. The first planks were

0   50   100   200 Miles.

Route .... De Soto
.... Followers.
Swamp. ⩊ ⩊ ⩊

TENN

ARKANSAS

TEXAS

LOUISIANA

Mississippi River

De Soto dies
1542

MISSISSIPPI

To Panuco Bay,
Mexico

Gulf of

Hernando De Sote

1539 – 1543. De So

SEE
N. CAROLINA
S. CAROLINA
ALABAMA
GEORGIA
FLORIDA
Pensacola Bay
Apalachee Bay
Tampa Bay
Mexico
From Cuba
in Florida
ied in 1542 ·

scarcely cut before he fell ill. The camp became silent and gloomy, and even the toughest soldiers looked worried and afraid. The army had always trusted Hernando. No other officer knew how to deal with Indian chieftains so well. Earnestly the Spaniards prayed that their captain might recover.

"Make sure you go down the river," Hernando whispered to Moscoso de Alvarado, the cavalier he named his successor. "When you build your settlement at Achusi, perhaps you will remember me."

Hernando de Soto died in that summer of 1542, at the age of forty-two. Grieving companions buried him in a lonely spot not far from their camp. Then, because they feared the Indians might remove his body, they decided that the river would make a safer resting place. They chose a stretch of water where the depth was sixty feet. There, in the middle of the night, they slipped Hernando's coffin into the Mississippi from the edge of a canoe.

The unhappy little army felt lost after their leader's death. They no longer wanted to go to Achusi and build a settlement. Officers and men decided foolishly to march back through Louisiana and reach Mexico by traveling overland. None of them had any idea how great the distance was. They did not know that a wide desert lay between them and the nearest Spanish frontiers in Mexico. Perhaps they hoped that during the journey they might find some country rich in gold and silver.

They reached Texas in September, after fighting and starving most of the way. In this new country they gorged themselves on bison meat and named the country *La Provincia de los Vaqueros,* or the district of the herdsmen. The farther westward they went, the more dry and dusty the land became. They passed sun-baked cliffs and sandy stretches where only a coarse grass could grow. The few Indians they met wandered from place to place in search of food. Cold winds swept across the wilderness at night, but no other sounds disturbed the silence of the desert.

The Spaniards felt lost and frightened. By October they knew they had made a mistake in trying to reach Mexico with most of their number obliged to make the journey on foot. They could go no farther in this direction. Their only remaining chance of safety was to hurry back to the Mississippi.

Somehow, in spite of incredible hardships, four hundred men remained alive to reach the western shore of the Mississippi in January, 1543, bringing with them seventy horses. Since Hernando's death, they had marched a thousand miles.

The Spaniards no longer looked anything like the army which had arrived in Tampa Bay three and a half years earlier. They were dressed in skins, and many of them were barefooted. Their hair and

beards were long and ragged. Their faces and bodies were thin and crisscrossed with the scars of wounds. Fifty more of them died of cold and sickness before the winter ended.

Officers and men labored to erect high wooden scaffoldings beside the river. They worked on these elevated platforms when warmer weather and melting snow caused the Mississippi to flood the surrounding land. They sawed planks, and made nails from their muskets with the help of a little forge. Paint for the hulls of seven barges was made by mixing resin with pig fat. The last few blankets and scraps of woolen cloth were unraveled to make packing for the seams of the vessels. When the countryside dried up, the men sawed planks from daylight to dark. Slowly the ships began to take shape.

All seven caravels, as the Spaniards called their boats, were finished in June. Now there came the

question of getting food for the voyage to Mexico.
A friendly Indian tribe provided a fair quantity of
corn. Pigs were killed and their salted flesh was
stored in kegs. Dead horses were preserved in the
same manner; the thirty now still alive were taken
aboard the ships. Only one Spaniard knew how to
make barrels. Every night he worked by the light
of resinous torches to prepare enough water con-

tainers for the voyage across the Caribbean Sea.

Several of the river tribes determined to make a last effort to destroy the Spaniards. Hundreds of their canoes chased the caravels down the Mississippi. They fired endless showers of arrows and tried to swarm aboard the ships whenever they could. The current and a light breeze helped the Spaniards to travel downstream at a speed of five

91

or six miles per hour. The Indian canoes had no difficulty in keeping up. Fighting nearly every day, tugging at the ponderous oars, trimming sails made of braided reeds, the Spaniards fled for twenty days down a thousand miles of river. During this terrible voyage they lost another fifty comrades, and the few remaining horses were killed. The canoes gave up the chase only when the caravels lumbered out of the river and into the Gulf of Mexico.

"We did not dare sail far out to sea," said one of the Spaniards, "because we did not know what course to steer in order to reach Cuba or Hispaniola. We had no charts and no compass, or other instruments, by which to find our position. We knew only that by going westward along the coast we must come at last to the coast of Mexico. Two days after we had left the Great River behind us, the water around our vessels still tasted fresh enough to drink."

The ships leaked and the water casks ran dry. The Spaniards hauled their vessels onto the beach, and while some of the men repaired the hulls, others refilled empty barrels at a nearby stream. Tropical storms nearly wrecked the caravels. One ship was actually hurled ashore on the crest of a monstrous wave. The crew escaped alive, but lost most of their remaining food, water, and weapons.

Fifty-five days after leaving their camp beside the Mississippi, the seven caravels reached the little Mexican fishing village of Panuco. The Spanish residents treated the crews in a kindly manner. They sent a messenger on horseback to Mexico City, bearing the news that the last of Hernando de Soto's army had returned alive. A month later, the Spaniards set out to walk the two hundred and fifty miles to the city, for there were no horses in Panuco to carry them. One of the soldiers described the journey in these words:

93

The onlookers were amazed and sorrowful to see us so sunburned and ragged, walking on foot, barelegged, and clothed in the skins of animals. The good people of the city hastened into the streets, led us back to their houses, brought food, and found us beds. Afterward they gave us presents of cloth and caps, knives, scissors, shoes, and all the other things we had need of. Many of them wept at seeing us in such poor condition.

Hernando's men recovered slowly from the hardships of their voyage. At first they were delighted to be in a civilized country, where they could eat good food and sleep at night without fear. Gradually, however, they began to forget the hard times they had known in Florida.

"Captain De Soto was right," they muttered among themselves. "Florida was a great country, where we might have built good homesteads for

ourselves. Our eyes were blinded by greed for silver and gold. We did not think of the fruitful soil beneath our feet. But now we are penniless and can never return. There will not come another leader like our Captain De Soto. Only he could see what wealth Florida might have brought to poor men out of Spain."

TUBA CITY AGENCY
BUREAU OF INDIAN AFFAIRS